SWEET AGONY

A writing manual of sorts
by Gene Olson

"*. . . it is better to write a bad limerick than to be able
to recite 'Paradise Lost.'*"

—A. S. Neill

WINDYRIDGE PRESS
780 Oxyoke Road / Grants Pass, Oregon 97526

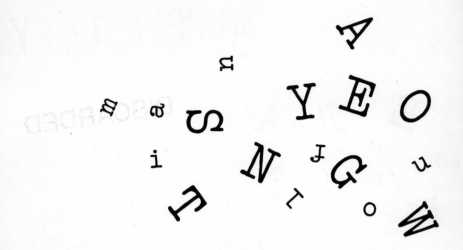

ISBN: 0-913366-03-X

Published by WINDYRIDGE PRESS
780 Oxyoke Road
Grants Pass, Oregon 97526

Printed in the United States of America

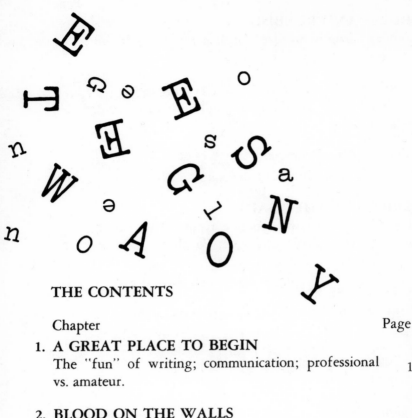

THE CONTENTS

Biographical Note:
Gene Olson, at this writing, lives on a hilltop in south-
ern Oregon (a *windy ridge*) and is now immersed in
publishing. His future homes are likely to be estab-
lished in Mexico, the northern California coast, Spain,
Greece and almost any other place where he can reason-
ably expect to learn the local language. His family con-
sists of a friendly wife, Joan, and an unfriendly Siamese
cat, Samisen, who also travel well (and frequently).

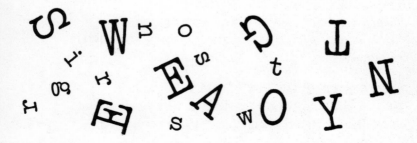

ACKNOWLEDGMENTS

Writing is a solitary occupation but this should not suggest that a writer must work without help. Foremost among those who helped with this book was my wife, Joan.

Others who aided in their special ways were Frank Arnich, Frank Bonham, Gloria Bonham, Keith Bonham, Gene Bray, Martin Cole, Owen Conway, John Cunningham, Clarice Foelker, Marcus Foelker, Walter Foelker, Joan Gleichman, Howard Hansen, Alice Huntsinger, Carol Huntsinger, Vance Huntsinger, Edna May Hill, Roberta Hutton, Alan Jochim, Margaret Knispel, Arthur Mann, Obena Olson, Alvin Pfahl, Brenda Pfahl, Susan Pfahl, Lorena Sample, Ray Sneddon, Walter Vernstrom, Harvey Dickey, Warren Talbot.

Thank you all.

Written permission to quote from copyrighted material has been granted by the following: Creative Writing Service, 149 Clinton Street, Brooklyn Heights, N.Y., *How They Murdered the Second R* by George Riemer; Native American Student Union, University of Oregon, "Indians' Prayer of Thanksgiving;" *Fortune,* article by Dr. Peter F. Drucker; Martin Cole, material about Col. Robert Short; Phillips Exeter Academy, *An Informal Manual of Style* by Alan H. Vrooman; title page quote from *Neill! Neill! Orange Peel!* by A. S. Neill, copyright 1972 Hart Publishing Company, Inc., New York; quote from column by Sydney J. Harris, courtesy Publishers-Hall Syndicate; Fog Index from *The Technique of Clear Writing* by Robert Gunning, McGraw-Hill, reprinted with written permission of Robert Gunning; Skagit Valley Publishing Co.

1.

A Great Place to Begin

You sit there, see, staring at that stark white piece of paper . . .

Which wouldn't be so bad except that . . . IT STARES BACK.

What's worse, it whines and wheedles and whinnies: "I want words. Give me words. Lots of words. Lovely words. Immortal words. *Don't leave me blank!*"

There, in a quivering capsule, is the writer's problem.

And that's what this book is about.

(Gee. Maybe it should be a bigger book.)

There's something I ought to explain about this book—it's not exactly organized. I didn't plan it to be disorganized; it just came out that way, perhaps because the whole thing is an accumulation of bits and pieces collected over a 20-year period of writing and teaching. From my present viewpoint, most of those bits and pieces seem to be pertinent to the problems of the struggling student writer. If I thought a bit or a piece might help, I threw it into the mix.

This is in the way of a warning that you mustn't expect this book to proceed primly from Point A to Point B and then finally to Point Z, without detours, like a dictionary or a grammar textbook. In writing this one, I operated more like Little Red Riding Hood wandering through the thick, dark woods of a writer's mind, coping with each new wolf as it leaped out of the underbrush. After all, there ought to be more than one way to get to Grandmother's house.

BAD TASTE STRIKES AGAIN

You will find the pronoun "I" used in this book a great many times. When overdone, this is considered bad taste.

I have overdone it.

Another much-used word in this book is "you." This is in better taste, I understand, but I suspect that I have run "you" into the ground as well.

Taste be hanged.

In this book, "I" am talking to "you" just as directly as if you were sitting in my parlor toasting your feet at my fire and eating my cheese and crackers. If the polite folks don't care for that, let them buy their own cheese and crackers.

You aren't expected to believe everything I say; I hope you won't. What has worked for me may not work for you. To write, a person must think for himself. Unless he does this, what he produces is nothing.

You hear me?

Writing is like falling in love in that we know it happens but no one is quite sure how it happens. Writing can be learned, but only the hard way, by doing it. You must make your own mistakes, learn what you can from them, then plunge on to make more mistakes.

If you go about this properly, both in falling in love and in writing, you won't make the same mistake more than three times and your new mistakes will be bigger and better than your old ones and you will learn more from them.

It's not that plenty of advice isn't available, both for writing and for falling in love. It's available in towering piles and the bulk of it isn't worth the powder to blow it to Stratford-on-Avon. I should know; I've sifted most of it through my brain. Through good luck or good sense, I've managed to ignore practically all of it, for a very good reason: *The advice simply didn't seem to work for me.*

You are no more likely to get a writing blueprint that works for you from somebody else than you are to get a plan for an ostrich house from the Home & Garden section of your local newspaper.

In my book there are no blueprints. This book is not a grammar text; there are already far too many of those. (Please, don't applaud in the middle of my act.) This book is not a guide to writing forms—short story, essay, etc. This book contains absolutely no instruction in use of a library card catalog, nor does it warn you against writing on both sides of the paper. I won't devote much space to telling you how to write; I'll devote much more space to showing you how *not* to write.

There won't be much in this book about *what* to write. That's important, for reasons I'll go into later.

There will be a great deal in this book about what might be called the psychology of writing. How does one get the creative juice flowing? How does one keep it flowing? How does one direct and discipline the mind for best results?

These are the kinds of things I'll be dealing with because I consider them the most important aspect of learning to write. Most of the remainder is practice.

A college president said in a newspaper interview: "Writing is a thinking process, and its study is a function of the psychologist. We have not made as much use of the psychologist in teaching English as we should have."

That man must have done some writing in his day.

A DOLLOP OF HOGWASH

At some time during your struggle to write, someone said or you read something like this:

"Writing is FUN!"

Or: "Creative writing is good for you!"

Or: "A writing person is a happy person!"

Once, twice, three times—NONSENSE. Anyone who believes this can't have done much serious writing. Nothing saps human energy—mental, emotional and *physical*—like sustained writing.

Even for a seasoned professional, the act is close to torture at times and he will often go to great lengths to avoid beginning it a moment sooner than necessary. A resourceful writer can postpone the beginning of writing for hours without really trying, for days with just a little effort and, if he is willing to strain a little, for months. I know of one writer who managed to avoid writing for two full years. (Anyone who achieves this kind of performance is entitled to refer to his difficulty as "writer's block.")

No one can write for you and there aren't any pat answers in the back of the book. Facing a blank sheet of paper, you are so alone that only you and the paper exist on a tiny, barren island. And you can sometimes feel the sand shifting . . .

This is at once the great charm of it and the terrible affliction of it.

Sweet agony . . .

I can give you a few pills for the pain but doubt not: The pain will always be there.

So why does anybody write anything?

I think I know. The fun is not in writing; the fun is in HAVING WRITTEN. I contend that few acts give human animals more and deeper emotional satisfaction than the act of writing. Those words spreading majestically over the paper are YOURS; they came out of YOUR teeming mind and no one else's. Your banner is unfurled before the world; you stand revealed, warts and all.

Writing is thinking and everyone knows how difficult *that* is. This piece of paper trembling in your hands proves that you have accomplished this wondrous deed. Now you are entitled to take the rest of the day off to enjoy the plaudits of the multitude who didn't write but just sat around like clods among the clover.

There, friend, right there and only there, is the fun of writing.

GOVERNMENT GLUE

Why write? It's only communication and who needs communication?

Apparently we all do. Cut off a human being from all contact with others of his kind and he may climb walls in an attempt to get out of his skull. Experiment after experiment has demonstrated this.

A fair amount of this country's worst writing flows like lukewarm glue out of the federal government. Oddly, some of the best books *about* writing have been produced by the U.S. Government Printing Office and some have been written by federal employees.

One such book is *Effective Revenue Writing,* by Dr. Calvin D. Linton, who is not a federal employee but a college teacher who has served as writing consultant to government agencies.

How important is communication? Dr. Linton lays it on the line for government writers:

> "Regardless of the intellectual powers we may possess, if we did not have the ability to communicate—to get ideas out of our heads into the heads of others—our salaries would abruptly stop. For all of us who work above the level of manual labor, communication skill is not *one* of the reasons we are hired; it is *the* reason. True, if we had no ideas to express we would be viewed with some concern by our superiors; but the sad fact is that an undeterminable but vast number of people have far better ideas than anyone knows. Their thoughts either beat about in their heads, finding no communication package in which to emerge; or they come out distorted and in fragments, jammed into words and sentences which do not exhibit them as they really are."

Dr. Peter F. Drucker, expert in business and industrial management, had this to say in a *Fortune Magazine* article:

> "If you work on a machine your ability to express yourself will be of little importance. But as soon as you move one step up from the bottom, your effectiveness depends on your ability to reach others through the spoken or the written word. And the further away your job is from manual work, the larger the organization of which you are an employee, the more important it will be that you know how to convey your thoughts in writing or speaking. In the very large organization, whether it is the government, the larger business corporation, or the Army, this ability to express oneself is perhaps the most important of all the skills a person can possess."

There are also those who argue that failures of communication are responsible for most of the world's troubles.

It has been demonstrated repeatedly down the long, bloody corridors of human history that groups of humans cut off from each other begin to fear each other, misunderstand each other, eventually hate each other and finally kill each other.

Mostly, we communicate with each other through words. Words express our thoughts, our hopes, our ambitions, our fears, our love, our hate. In a world where a politician can push a button and zap us all into the wild blue nowhere, it might be wise for us to learn how to use words better. Otherwise, somebody some day might mistake love for hate. Both, after all, are four-letter words.

You may think about that until recess.

LIONS WITH BIG MOUTHS

The basic problem facing a professional writer is much like that facing a student in school. The student is more fortunate in that he must solve the problem only once a week, or once a month, or possibly only once a semester.

A professional must put his head into that lion's mouth every working day.

The arena is littered with losers, mostly headless. The dropout rate is high among both students and professionals. A professional who survives has learned some tricks and some of those tricks can be applied as easily to the writing of a 500-word composition as to a full-length novel.

Does the professional have anything to say to the amateur? This book is an attempt to find out.

At the risk of becoming tedious, let's say again: This is no book for turning a lazy clod into a passable writer. There *are* writing books for lazy clods; most of them consist of neat little rules numbered from "1" to infinity.

There are even books which promise to teach you how to become a rich and famous novelist merely by following a prescription mailed down from Mt. Sinai.

This is not that kind of book, either.

This is a book for those concerned persons who understand the need for better written communication, who are stimulated by the awesome challenge of writing, who above all are willing to work at it.

Who above all are willing to work at it . . .

Now that we've been introduced, shall we dance?

SOMETHING TO READ

Go back in time a century and a half. You have been invited to a duel. A real one, complete with blood. Not as a spectator, unfortunately; as a *participant*. You don't want to do it; you aren't really that mad at anybody. Besides, you know better than to let yourself get shot in a pertinent place.

So you decide to write a letter to your challenger that will leave him laughing on the floor and will make your reputation as a devastating writer in the bargain. Tough, huh?

But not impossible. Judge Breckinridge, father of John C. Breckinridge, vice president under Buchanan from 1857 to 1861, was challenged to a duel to the death by a British officer in the late 1790s. Judge Breckinridge replied:

"Sir; I have two objections to this duel matter. The one is lest I should hurt you; the other, lest you should hurt me. I do not see any good it would do me to put a bullet through any part of your body. I could make no use of you when dead for any culinary purpose, as I could a rabbit or a turkey . . . for though your flesh might be delicate and tender, yet it wants that firmness and consistency which takes and retains salt. At any rate, it would not be fit for long sea voyages. You might make a good barbecue, it is true, being of the nature of a racoon or an opossum, but people are not in the habit of barbecuing anything human now. As to your hide, it is not worth taking off, being little better than that of a two-year-old colt. As to myself, I do not much like to stand in the way of anything that is harmful. I am under the apprehension that you might hit me. That being the case, I think it most advisable to stay at a distance. If you want to try your pistols, take some object—a tree or a barn door—about my dimensions, and if you hit that, send me word. I shall then acknowledge that if I had been in the same place you would have killed me in a duel.

> "I have the honor to be,
> Sir,
> Your hmbl. & obt. servant,
> John Breckinridge"

Isn't that beautiful? If a few presidents and kings and premiers and archdukes could have called upon writers of the caliber of Breckinridge, some gory wars might have been avoided. It's hard to kill people when you are laughing.

Pen vs. sword—bet on the pen.

SOMETHING TO THINK ABOUT

> *"The crossover of a thought from mind to paper is an utterly lonely passage, and no amount of tender loving handholding care will make it less so."*

> —George Riemer

"But only through initially painful self-criticism and through intense concentration and effort can we slowly begin to develop habits of clear writing. I have never known a good writer, nor ever heard of one, who wrote without suffering. Old Dr. Johnson, whose style has that perfect marble-like solidity of a superbly carved statue, swore that it took the pressure of actual hunger to spur him into the anguish of covering a clean sheet of paper with words."

—Dr. Calvin D. Linton

2.

Blood on the Walls

There are about eleven million words (11,000,000) in the English language. Each of those eleven million words is composed of combinations of 26 letters of the alphabet. Those 26 letters make up most of the keyboard of a standard typewriter.

If you punch the right keys among those 26, you automatically form the right words out of those eleven million and transform your nothing-nobody self into the world's greatest writer of the world's greatest book—rich, famous, immortal.

It's all there in the 26 letters of the English alphabet. Just punch the right keys at the right time.

So? The typical writer of a school composition doesn't plan to get rich from it. What he or she wants to do is knock his or her teacher on his or her shoulder blades with a devastating batch of those 26 letters—and get an "A" in red pencil.

And that isn't easy.

The English writer, Oscar Wilde, came out of his writing room late one day and murmured, "I spent all morning putting in a comma and all afternoon taking it out."

An Irish writer, Flannery O'Connor, once told a group of students: "Every morning between nine and 12, I go to my room and sit before a piece of paper. Many times, I just sit for three hours with no ideas coming to me. But I know one thing: if an idea does come between nine and 12, I am there ready for it."

Another writer described the act of writing as "fighting an angel." Some people hold the silly notion that good writing is easy because it looks easy. The words flow smoothly off the page into the reader's brain, so they surely must flow onto the page just as creamily. Not so; the only easy writing is *bad* writing and bad writing remains easy only until it strikes a baffled reader head-on.

Plunging off a 40-story building while playing "Yellow Rose of Texas" on the harmonica may look easy, too, but you would be wise to keep an open mind until you've tried it.

All the way . . .

BUTTERFLIES, ANYONE?

Student writers often get discouraged and moan: "Why, after writing a composition a week for two years, can't I write like John Steinbeck?"

There are many professional writers who have ground out tens of millions of words who can't write like John Steinbeck. Even John Steinbeck had days when he couldn't write like John Steinbeck.

There is no more demanding task than writing. No matter how long one works at it, no matter how many words are produced, room for improvement will always remain. Herein lies the ultimate frustration of writing; herein also lies its bittersweet charm and challenge. It's like chasing butterflies in a world where there are always more butterflies, each new batch prettier than the last.

Writing and talking are both means of communication. No argument there. Also, both use words. How, then, can they be so different?

It is a striking fact that many persons who talk easily tend to sweat blood when they try to write. Why? Words are words, aren't they?

Sometimes. There is often a great difference between a person's talk and that same person's writing. Talk is usually relaxed and warm and breezy and a little disjointed. In a word, informal. Writing, on the other hand, is often stiff and cold and lifeless. In a word, formal.

For most persons, talking must be easier than writing because they do so much more of it. Talking may be easier because it doesn't ask words to carry the entire message. Watch a person talking; he will cock an eyebrow, smile, sneer, wave his hands, stamp his feet, grunt, snort, even jump up and down if it will help inoculate his listener with the message. In comparison, a writer seems like a hopeless cripple.

Actually, though, he isn't. The writer can work slowly and carefully; the talker must jabber like mad to fill that screaming void of silence (or lose the floor). The writer can revise in a cool afterglow, snipping out bad words, sliding in good. The talker often must speak first, think later.

Which can be dangerous, even if one isn't a politician.

Yet there is something about talking that seems so effortless and natural, perhaps because it began with the first cry from the cradle. The words flow out in a steady stream, echo against the far wall and disappear. If you wish, you can even deny them and only a tape recorder can call you a liar.

Putting words on paper is something else. Words on paper lie there in mute splendor, staring coldly back, silently labelling you an idiot or a genius.

"Did I say *that?*"

"Of course you did. There it is, right there on the paper. *You said it.* It says so right there."

The act of writing, even in the privacy of one's own room, seems like a public act, almost like giving a speech in a crowded auditorium. Once impaled on paper, words may pass from hand to hand and eye to eye forever—or at least until the print smears and the paper yellows.

You've heard the warning: "Say whatever you want but don't put anything on paper!"

Writing commits the writer in a way that talking does not commit the talker. I wonder if this explains why students who will talk until their teeth fall out will write only under threat of the whip. Writing, we know, is only thinking on paper. Talking should be nothing more than thinking out loud, but too often in this yak-yak world, it is just talking.

Most of us would function better if our writing were more like our talk and if our talk were more like our writing.

If you happen to be the kind of person who needs a clear goal, there's a dandy.

Psychologists have decided that many persons resist writing because writing reveals character. The reluctant writer's subconscious mind may be planting the fear: *How will you look on paper?*